FINGERPRINT
BUGS

by Bobbie Nuytten

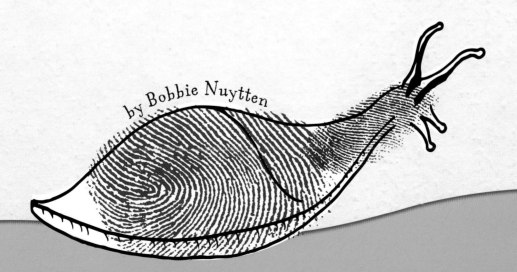

PICTURE WINDOW BOOKS
a capstone imprint

Welcome to the fun world of fingerprint art!

Make your own crawling bugs and flying insects with your fingers! Did you know that a fingerprint can be the start of a piece of art? Use the following pages to help you make your own bug creations!

Here's what you'll need to get started:

ink

Use an ink pad that's labeled washable. You can pick any size or shape you like. You can even use your favorite color!

pens

Find a pen or marker with a fine tip. An artist pen from a craft store will work too. Use the pen to add shapes and lines to your fingerprints.

paper

Pick the paper you like best. Smooth computer paper will show the lines in your fingerprints. You can also use thicker paper from a craft store.

FINGERPRINT TIPS

Use different parts of your finger to change the bug's size and shape.

Use the center of your finger or thumb to make oval shapes with lots of lines.

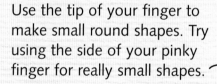

Use the tip of your finger to make small round shapes. Try using the side of your pinky finger for really small shapes.

Use the side of your finger to make long, skinny shapes.

Press down hard on the paper to make your fingerprint darker. A lighter touch will make your fingerprint lighter.

busy bee

chirping cricket

silly snail

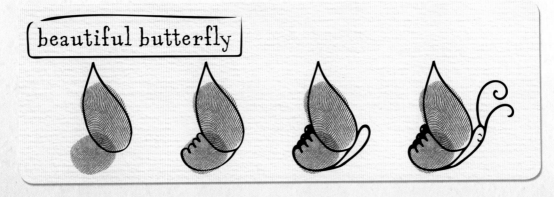

beautiful butterfly

working ant

hungry caterpillar

spotted ladybug

jumping grasshopper

flying June bug

fluttering moth

hanging spider

glowing firefly

8

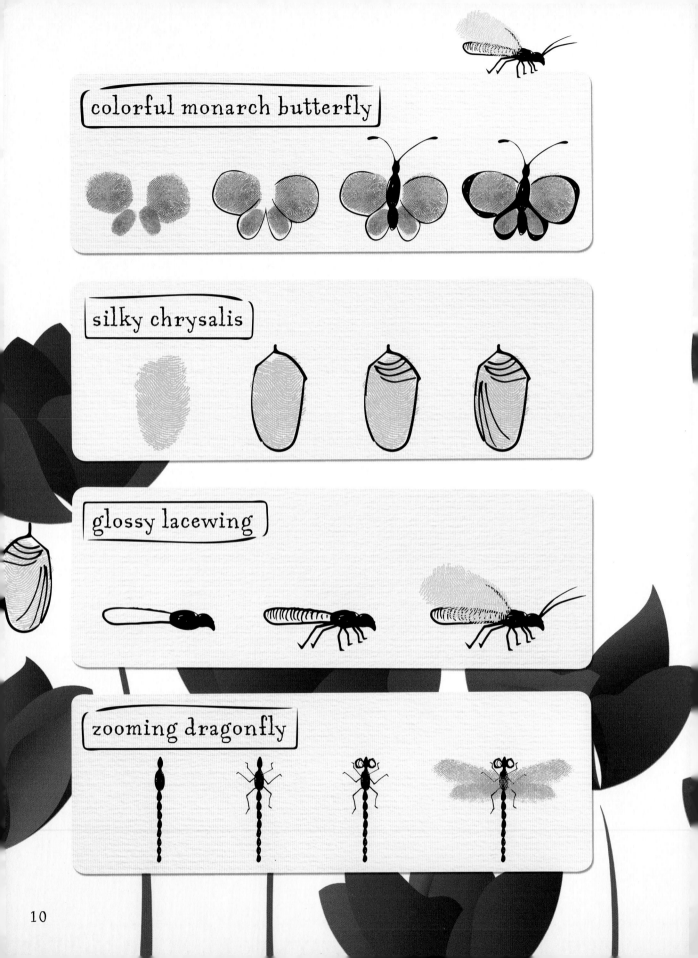

colorful monarch butterfly

silky chrysalis

glossy lacewing

zooming dragonfly

10

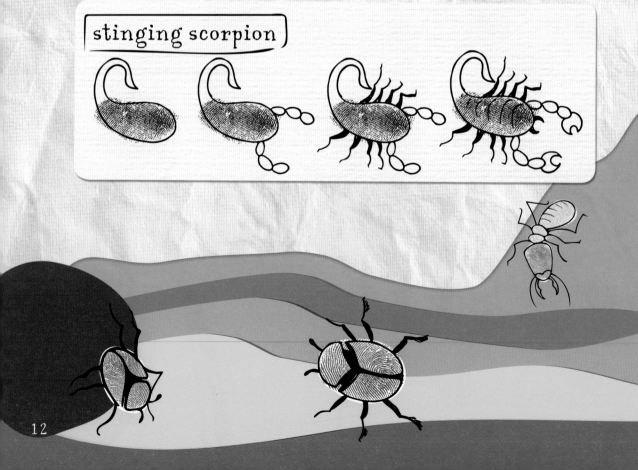

munching termite

swimming water strider

darting damselfly

14

biting mosquito

slow slug

bright lantern bug

striking praying mantis

horned Hercules beetle

fuzzy silk moth caterpillar

hiding flower spider

chomping hornworm

crawling potato beetle

18

hovering Sphinx moth

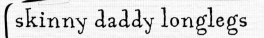
skinny daddy longlegs

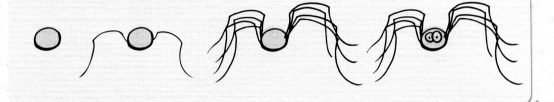

slippery silverfish

buzzing housefly

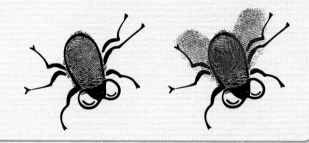

wiggling centipede

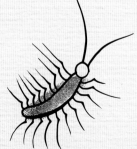
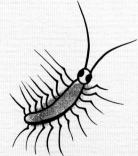

20

21

growing cicada nymph

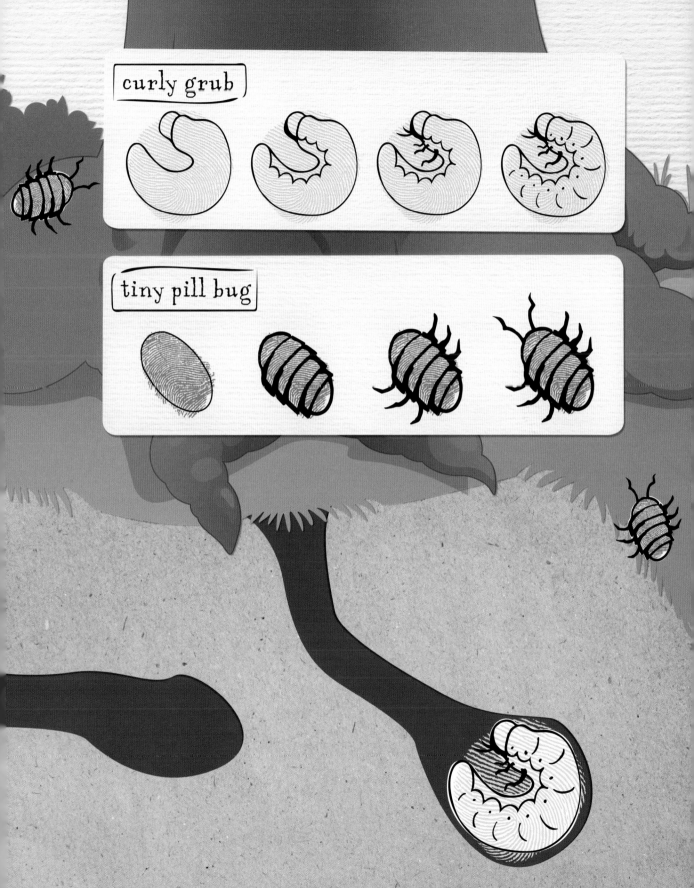

curly grub

tiny pill bug

For Lexi and Mia—you taught me to see masterpieces in every scribble.

About the Illustrator

Bobbie Nuytten lives in southern Minnesota with her husband, two young daughters, two golden retrievers, and cat. She has been a designer for over 14 years, focusing on children's books for the last 12 years. Bobbie has always been an avid crafter. In recent years she has been interested in making art and crafts accessible and fun for kids, especially her daughters.

Read More

Gray, Peter. *How to Draw Butterflies and Other Insects.* How to Draw Animals. New York: PowerKids Press, 2014.

Guillain, Charlotte. *Get Drawing!* Dream It, Do It! Chicago: Capstone Raintree, 2014.

Regan, Lisa. *Bugs.* Let's Draw. New York: Windmill Books, 2011.

Internet Sites

FactHound offers a safe, fun way to find Internet sites related to this book. All of the sites on FactHound have been researched by our staff.

Here's all you do:

Visit *www.facthound.com*

Type in this code: 9781479586844

Check out projects, games and lots more at
www.capstonekids.com

Editor: Michelle Hasselius
Designer: Bobbie Nuytten
Creative Director: Nathan Gassman
Production Specialist: Lori Blackwell

The illustrations in this book were created with pen and ink, and digital collage.

Picture Window Books are published by Capstone,
1710 Roe Crest Drive, North Mankato, Minnesota 56003
www.mycapstone.com

Library of Congress Cataloging-in-Publication Data
Cataloging-in-publication information is on file with the Library of Congress.
ISBN 978-1-4795-8684-4 (library binding)
ISBN 978-1-4795-8688-2 (eBook PDF)

Photographs and background elements from Shutterstock.

Printed in the United States of America in North Mankato, Minnesota.
102015   009221CGS16

Look for all four titles to find more ways to have fun with fingerprints!

FINGERPRINT
ANIMALS

FINGERPRINT
BUGS

FINGERPRINT
CHARACTERS

FINGERPRINT
VEHICLES